The Lectin free cookbook

Healthy and delicious recipes for every brand of electric pressure cooker

Dr. Steven banks

Table of contents

CHAPTER-1: LECTIN FREE DIET BASIC
WHAT ARE LECTINS?

Lectins fall under that category of proteins which acts as a binding force between cell membranes. They are basically sugar-binding and are the 'glycol' portion of the glycoconjugates on the cell membranes. It aids the cells to bind together without the aid of immune system and is the key factor in the cell-cell linkages.

Lectins are considerably high in raw grains and legumes and is generally found in that specific portion of the seed called cotyledon which becomes the leave when the plant grows and sprouts. The amount of lectin in food is almost constant but the cross breeding and genetic changes in plants have impacted the amount of lectin in plants.

Lectins are also responsible for being defensive maneuver in plants against insects, pets and other microorganisms attacking them. They are also responsible for a medium for seeds to remain in their original form after passing through animal's digestive systems for their later dispersal. Lectins are not digested by the human digestive system and they are introduced to the blood without any alterations. Lectins are also carrying nitrogen which is very necessary for plant growth. Lectin is mostly found in many parts of the plant but it is the seed which is usually consumed in a larger quantity.

The effective way for lowering the number of lectins in plants is considered to be those cooking techniques which involve moist heat. Cooking is also effective in breaking down certain plant starch into much simpler forms of carbohydrates. Lectins are considerably attached to these carbohydrates and are effectively removed from the body before causing any negative or harmful effects. It is not recommended to use slow cookers for preparing kidney beans because of the lower temperatures not effective enough to remove lectins. The effects methods and techniques to remove lectins are as follows:

- Deseeding
- Fermentation:

   Fermentation is the process that allows the bacteria beneficial for the body for digestion and converting various harmful substances. This is considered as the reason to why many healthy people continue using fermented soy products like tempeh, miso, natto and tamari. The fermented forms of certain veggies like cabbage etc. carry lesser anti nutrients. People having a history of grain consumption have considerably applied fermentation to treat grains. This method doesn't remove all the lectins rather a few hardcore lectins remain unchanged in this process.

- Peeling
- Boiling
- Pressure cooking and Soaking:

The reason for soaking, boiling and rinsing of beans is due to reduce the lectins. This has been in application for a longer time period. To reduce the lectins effectively, soak legumes and beans overnight and change the water various times. Afterwards rinse and drain them again before finally cooking them. In addition to this, the introduction of baking soda to the soaking water can considerably neutralize the lectins even more.

- Sprouting

Seeds, beans and grains when sprouted get their lectin content reduced. This process is directly proportional to the time span of sprouting. In a few odd cases like that of alfalfa, the lectin activity is enhanced. Lectins are present in the seed coat of some grains and seeds. When it is germinated, the coat gets metabolized and thus removes the lectins.

Apart from their harmful effects on the body, lectins are also credited to be a positive thing. A little number of lectins aid the good bacteria present in the digestive systems of the human body. They are also considered to be highly effective in identifying and diagnosing cancer according to a research. They are also being researched upon for their effectiveness in slowing down the rate of multiplication of cancer cells. They are also being medically researched upon by scientists as a treatment and cure for illness and diseases caused by certain viruses, bacteria and fungus.

WHAT IS WRONG WITH LECTINS?

They have known to be impacting health in many ways. It ranges from increased risk of chronic diseases to digestion system complications. They are known to be responsible for the clustering together of red blood cells. They are also known to be considered and categorized as anti-nutrients as they are responsible for blocking the absorption and digestion of certain nutrients. They are also responsible for causing stomach related medical complications when plant related foods are consumed uncooked. They are also the reason for the dangers caused by undercooked legumes.

Phytohemagglutinin is the lectin which is found in red kidney beans. It may cause severe diarrhea, nausea and vomiting which is commonly known as red kidney bean poisoning and is caused due to the consumption of undercooked or raw kidney beans. As per the statement and research of United States Food & Drug Administration (FDA), a mere four kidney beans can cause the kidney bean positioning if consumed undercooked or in raw form.

FOODS RECOMMENDED EATING

As per Dr. Gundry, the following foods are known to be effective and are recommended for those people who want to reduce and limit their lectin intake befittingly:

- Meats (pasture raised)

- Milk (A2)

- Sweet Potatoes (cooked)

- Veggies (leafy and green)

- Veggies (cruciferous) i.e. Brussels sprouts and broccoli etc.

- Onions and garlic

- Asparagus

- Mushrooms

- Celery

- Olive oil (extra virgin) or olives

- Avocado

FOODS RECOMMENDED AVOIDING

As per Dr. Gundry, the following foods are known to be high in lectins and are recommended to be avoided for those people who want to reduce and limit their lectin intake befittingly:

- Squash

- Legumes i.e. peas, beans, peanuts and lentils etc.

- Veggies (nightshade) such as peppers, eggplants, tomatoes and potatoes. Important note: studies show that tomatoes with seeds and skin have most lectin so using roman tomatoes would be a great idea with least skin and seeds if you so want to use tomatoes.

- Fruits (it should be duly noted that in-season fruits are allowed if consumed in a moderate rate).

- Grains (in case of grain consumption, the lectin free diet plan recommends products manufactured from white flour instead of those manufactured from wheat).

STRICTLY AVOIDED FOODS

The following foods are recommended to be strictly avoided at any cost while being on the lectin free diet plan according to Dr. Gundry:

- A1 milk
- Meat (from animals fed on corn)
- Corn

LECTIN-FREE DIET AND ITS BENEFITS

The person who is the reason for the popularization of the lectin free diet is Dr. Steven Gundry. He is a former cardiologist and heart surgeon and has switched his focus and attention to supplement and food-based medication. According to him, lectins are the major harmful ingredients found in the American diet. To tackle the issue, he has written a book which is based upon how to avoid and reduce lectins, alternatives for lectin carrying foods and recipes. According to the content of the book, the lectin free diet plan from Dr. Gundry is considered to be effective in boosting health and weight loss. The book is also having supplements developed by the author which are sold under the brand 'Gundry MD'.

BENEFITS

There are numerous benefits of the lectin free diet plan and is very effective in weight loss and other health improvements. Some of them are as follows:

- In the opinion of some scientists, lectins are considerably harmful for health and are the reason for inflammation. They are also considered to be causing autoimmune diseases like diabetes, rheumatoid arthritis and even celiac disease. Using the lectin free diet plan, the users can evidently avoid these harmful medical complications caused by lectin intake.
- The white germ lectin is known for causing drastic effects on the immune system by causing a considerable increase in inflammation. Using the lectin free diet plan, the users can evidently avoid these harmful medical complications caused by lectin consumption.
- Inflammation for a longer time span is considered to be causing serious medical complications and diseases like cancer, depression and even cardiac complications like heart attacks etc. Using the lectin free diet plan, the users can evidently avoid these harmful medical complications caused by lectin consumption.
- Lectins are responsible for the easiness for bacteria and other toxins to overlap the gut barrier. According to scientific research, whole grains carry antioxidants which are known to be effective in fighting inflammation. This might be the considered as the potentially harmful effects of lectins.

- A lectin free diet if followed can cause a considerable reduction in inflammation. But, further research is required to confirm the effectiveness of lectin free diet in this regard.

TIPs

- Consume natural foods like cooked tubers, leafy greens, avocados, cruciferous veggies, olive and extra virgin olive oils.
- Use a pressure cooker for cooking.
- Always deseed and peel your fruits and vegetables.
- Always prefer white grains over brown.
- Divide your shopping list into groups to avoid it becoming a financial burden.
- Shop at wholesale clubs or online stores for your lectin free shopping list.

RISKs

With numerous benefits, the lectin free diet also brings along some cons. A few of its cons are as follows:

1. It is a restrictive plan and can be hard to follow for a longer time period.
2. It removes or limits certain nutritious foods like beans, whole grains and even some veggies.

According to medical and scientific research, the consumption of whole grains can be beneficial in reducing the risk of cardiac diseases, cancer and even diabetes. There are many health benefits of fruits and veggies consumption. Their high consumption may reduce the dangers of various medical complications including cardiac issues, lungs related medical issues and even considerable weight loss alongside reducing the risk of cancer. The lectin free diet is considered to be hard to follow by vegans and vegetarians as legumes, seeds, nuts and whole grains are the source for plant-based protein. They are also the sources for provision of dietary fiber. There will be a risk of constipation while consuming a lectin free diet because of the lower intake of dietary fibers. The plan may also be expensive and hard to tackle financially because of the inclusion of pasture raised meats, highly priced supplements and special milks.

CHAPTER2: ELECTRIC PRESSURE COOKER:

Pressure cookers are not a new invention and have been in use for a long time now. They have made cooking very convenient, considerably lowered the cooking time and are very effective for working class of the society. From cooking stew to roasting meat or preparing beans, every cooking operation has become considerably easy with the advent of pressure cookers. With everything getting modernized and electric, the pressure cooker industry was also revolutionized with the advent of electric pressure cooker. The new electric pressure cooker is excellent in performing almost all cooking tasks and has perfectly replaced the older versions of pressure cooker with the same or even quicker cooking time. They have taken the cooking industries by a storm and various restaurants are switching to them gradually with all the convenience and advantages they offer. Some of the advantages of electric pressure cooker are as follows:

ADVANTAGES OF USING AN ELECTRIC PRESSURE COOKER:

- Cooking time is reduced by almost 90 percent
- Much convenient and time saving than conventional pressure cookers
- Better digestibility
- Nutrient retention is up to 90 percent
- Fewer cooking side effects
- They have specially designed automatic steam mechanism which vents steam before they reach unsafe levels. This quick release feature is an additional pro to the older conventional designed pressure cooker. It eradicates the worrying about steam venting.
- They have a very safe usage and prevent any harm to the user alongside providing a steady pressure and temperature inside the pot. The locking lid feature doesn't allow the lid to be removed unless the pressure inside the pot drops to a safer value.
- They are much cleaner than conventional pressure cookers like the stove top cookers. Their pots are made from non-stick coated materials and stainless steel.

CHAPTER 3: FAQ

1. What are lectins?

   Lectins fall under that category of proteins which acts as a binding force between cell membranes. They are basically sugar-binding and are the 'glycol' portion of the glycoconjugates on the cell membranes. It aids the cells to bind together without the aid of immune system and is the key factor in the cell-cell linkages. They are known to cause digestion complications and other medical issues.

2. Should lectin be avoided?

   The lectin free diet helps some people and is not effective for everybody having stomach issues. In case of serious issues, you should consult a proper doctor or dietitian for expert opinion. It is up to the user and his needs which is going to define whether to avoid lectins or not.

3. What is the lectin free diet?

   The lectin free diet removes all the high-lectin foods like quinoa, grains and legumes etc. They also recommend avoiding dairy, non-seasonal fruits and conventionally raised poultry etc. It recommends low-lectin foods like veggies (leafy greens) like broccoli and cauliflower, mushrooms, nuts etc.

4. Is the lectin free diet effective in weight loss?

   Yes, the lectin free diet is very effective in weight loss alongside many other medical benefits. It has lowered the risk of cardiovascular diseases and metabolism syndrome.

5. Why Butter is considered Ok but dairy isn't?

   It is evident to note that dairy products are high in lectin content. But, grass fed butter is not high in lectin. Milk produced by grain feeding is having higher amount of lectin as compared to grass fed. Homogenized and pasteurized milk has lower SIgA as compared to the other. SIgA groups with harmful lectins and is a immunoglobulin found in raw milk.

CHAPTER 4: BREAKFAST RECIPES

EGG MUFFINS

Preparation Time: 10 minutes
Cooking Time: 15 minutes
Servings: 4

Ingredients:

- 4 eggs
- ¼ teaspoon lemon pepper seasoning
- 1 green onion, diced
- 4 slices grass-fed bacon, precooked

Method:

1. Add 1½ cups water and place the rack in the cooker pot.
2. In a mixing bowl, break eggs and whisk well. Add all the other ingredients and divide the muffin batter equally in muffin mounds.
3. Place these muffins on the rack or metal trivet. Cook this on high pressure on 8 minutes.
4. Do a natural pressure release and remove the cooked muffins carefully.

Nutritional Value:

- *Calories 141*
- *Total Fat 11 g*
- *Saturated Fat 3.9 g*
- *Cholesterol 122 mg*
- *Sodium 444 mg*
- *Total Carbs 2.2 g*
- *Fiber 0.5 g*
- *Sugar 1.3 g*
- *Protein 9.3 g*
- *Potassium 86 mg*

GINGER BREAD

Preparation Time: 5 minutes
Cooking Time: 2 minutes
Servings: 2

Ingredients:

- 1 teaspoon ginger, grounded
- ½ teaspoon cinnamon
- ¼ teaspoon cloves
- 2 tablespoons butter, softened
- ¼ teaspoon nutmeg
- 4 teaspoons maple flavored erythritol syrup
- 1 teaspoon apple cider vinegar
- 1 tablespoon water
- 2 tablespoons coconut flour
- 2 tablespoons cassava flour
- 1 teaspoon baking powder
- large eggs, lightly beaten

Method:

1. Take a bowl and add in the butter along with ginger, cinnamon, coconut flour, baking powder, cassava flour, and spices.
2. Next, in the same bowl combine in the syrup with cider vinegar; water, and egg.
3. Continue beating it briskly with a fork until batter is silky and steady.
4. Transfer the mixture into a mini bread loaf pan.
5. Place a steam basket in the pressure cooker and add in 2 cups of water in it.
6. Carefully place the mini loaf pan straight without tilting.
7. Close the lid and turn the heat to high and when it reaches pressure, turn the flame to minimum and cook for 6-8 minutes.
8. Pressure release naturally and use a toothpick to check whether the bread is cooked or not; if the toothpick comes out clean, then bread is done.
9. Serve hot.

Nutritional Value:

- Calories 215
- Total Fat 16.2 g
- Saturated Fat 9.3 g
- Cholesterol 124 mg
- Sodium 126 mg
- Total Carbs 24.2 g
- Fiber 7.4 g
- Sugar 10.4 g
- Protein 5.5 g
- Potassium 334 mg

VANILLA MUFFIN

Preparation Time: 2 minutes
Cooking Time: 12 minutes
Servings: 2

Ingredients:

- 2 large pastured eggs, beaten
- 4 tablespoons extra virgin olive oil
- 4 teaspoons granular monk, fruit sweetener
- 2 tablespoons coconut flour
- 2 tablespoons seasonal fruit
- 2 tablespoons tiger nut flour
- 1 teaspoon baking powder
- 1 teaspoon vanilla
- ¼ teaspoon sea salt

Method:

1. Take a bowl and mix in olive oil along with coconut flour, tiger nut flour, sweetener, baking powder, vanilla, and salt.
2. Next, add in the egg and beat with a fork until batter is silky smooth.
3. Now, gently fold in the fruits of your choice.
4. Transfer the mixture into a mini bread loaf pan.
5. Place a steam basket in the pressure cooker and add in 2 cups of water in it.
6. Carefully place the mini loaf pan straight without tilting.
7. Close the lid and turn the heat to high and when it reaches pressure, turn the flame to minimum and cook for 12 minutes.
8. Pressure release naturally and use a toothpick to check whether the bread is cooked or not; if the toothpick comes out clean, then the muffin is done.
9. Serve warm or cold as per your choice.

Nutritional Value:

- *Calories 347*
- *Total Fat 32.6 g*

- *Saturated Fat 5.5 g*
- *Cholesterol 215 mg*
- *Sodium 302 mg*
- *Total Carbs 10.2 g*
- *Fiber 1.4 g*
- *Sugar 6.1 g*
- *Protein 6.2 g*
- *Potassium 315 mg*

ALMOND FLOUR BISCUITS

Preparation Time: 5 minutes
Cooking Time: 20 minutes
Servings: 8

Ingredients:

- 3 cups almond flour, blanched
- 2 teaspoons baking powder
- 1 teaspoon kosher salt
- 6 tablespoons cold butter, diced
- 6 tablespoons coconut cream
- 2 eggs

Method:

1. In a bowl mix together, almond flour with salt and baking powder.
2. Next, take some cold diced butter and mix it with the flour.
3. Keep on cutting the butter and mixing in the flour till the dough is crumbly.
4. Make a hole in the center of the bowl and put in the eggs and cream together; mix both of the ingredients with light hands.
5. Next, incorporate the egg cream mixture with the rest of the flour and mix until soft dough is formed.
6. Make balls out of the cookie dough and then make cookies out of each ball. Make sure not to flatten the dough.
7. Grease a baking tray and put the cookies over it.
8. Place a trivet in the pressure cooker.
9. Carefully place the baking tray the pressure cooker without tilting.
10. Close the lid and turn the heat to high and when it reaches pressure, turn the flame to minimum and cook for 20 minutes.
11. Pressure release naturally and see whether the cookies are cooked properly by seeing the sides of the cookies.
12. Serve warm or cold as per your choice.

Nutritional Value:

- Calories 159
- Total Fat 15.6 g
- Saturated Fat 8.4 g
- Cholesterol 64 mg
- Sodium 373 mg
- Total Carbs 2.7 g
- Fiber 1 g
- Sugar 0.5 g
- Protein 3 .2g
- Potassium 173mg

KOREAN STYLE STEAMED EGGS

Preparation Time: 5 minutes
Cooking Time: 5 minutes
Servings: 2

Ingredients:

- ¼ teaspoon salt
- 1/2 cup cold water
- 2 teaspoons scallions, chopped
- ¼ teaspoon sesame seeds
- 2 large pasture eggs
- ¼ teaspoon garlic powder
- ¼ teaspoon pepper

Method:

1. Take a bowl and whisk together egg with some water.
2. Next, strain the egg mixture over a fine mesh strainer into a heat proof bowl.
3. Now, add 1 cup of water in an inner pot of the electric pressure cooker and place a trivet inside it.
4. Place the egg bowl over the trivet and close the lid of the cooker while setting the temperature on "Manual" High for almost 6 minutes.
5. After the timer goes off release the pressure naturally and transfer the bowl onto the table.
6. Serve immediately.

Nutritional Value:

- *Calories 75*
- *Total Fat 4.7 g*
- *Saturated Fat 1.5 g*
- *Cholesterol 215 mg*
- *Sodium 356 mg*
- *Total Carbs 1.6 g*
- *Fiber 0.2 g*

- Sugar 0.1 g
- Protein 6.2 g
- Potassium 14 mg

HARD BOILED EGGS

Preparation Time: 1 minute
Cooking Time: 5 minutes
Servings: 2

Ingredients:

- 4 large pasture eggs
- 1 cup water

Method:

1. In the inner pot of the electric pressure cooker put in some water and then place a trivet in it.
2. Next, put the eggs over the trivet and then close the lid of the cooker along with closing the vent valve.
3. Select "Manual" and set the pressure on high for 5 minutes for the eggs to cook fully hard.
4. After the timer goes off, release the pressure naturally and open the lid of the cooker.
5. Take the eggs out and place them in the bowl of cold water.
6. Peel them and enjoy eating!

Nutritional Value:

- Calories 140
- Total Fat 9 g
- Saturated Fat 3 g
- Cholesterol 430 mg
- Sodium 130 mg
- Total Carbs 2 g
- Fiber 0 g
- Sugar 0 g
- Protein 12 g
- Potassium 0 mg

GLORY MUFFINS

Preparation Time: 10 minutes
Cooking Time: 40 minutes
Servings: 6

Ingredients:

- 1 cup sweet potato, mashed
- 1 cup raisins
- 1 cup walnuts, chopped
- ½ cup honey
- 2 teaspoons cinnamon
- 4 pasture eggs
- 1 cup coconut, shredded
- ¼ cup carrot, shredded
- 1 ½ cup almond flour
- 2 teaspoons vanilla extract
- 2 teaspoons baking powder

Method:

1. Take a bowl and mix in all the ingredients of the glory muffins.
2. Take a medium muffin tray and grease it using cooking spray.
3. Divide the batter among the cups.
4. Take a pressure cooker and set a trivet in it.
5. Place the muffin mound over the trivet making sure that it does not tilt.
6. Close the lid of the pressure cooker and allow it to cook for about 30 minutes.
7. After the timer goes off, allow the pressure to release naturally and then remove the lid.
8. Use a toothpick to check whether the muffin is cooked or not; if the toothpick comes out clean, then the muffin is done.
9. Transfer the tray onto the table and allow the muffins to cool down.
10. Finally, release the muffins from the tray and serve.

Nutritional Value:

- Calories 460
- Total Fat 23.4 g
- Saturated Fat 5.9 g
- Cholesterol 96 mg
- Sodium 45 mg
- Total Carbs 38.4 g
- Fiber 4 g
- Sugar 27.6 g
- Protein 8.4 g
- Potassium 466 mg

CHAPTER 5: SNACKS
ROASTED WHOLE GARLIC

Preparation Time: 5 minutes
Cooking Time: 20 minutes
Servings: 6
Ingredients:

- 3 large garlic bulbs.
- 1 cup water

Method:

1. Slice off ¼ of the garlic bulb form the top keeping the bulb intact.
2. Prepare the pressure cooker pot by adding water and place the rack on it.
3. Keep the garlic bulb on the rack and pressure cook for 5-6 minutes on high pressure.
4. Do a natural pressure release and remove the soft garlic very carefully.
5. Keep this in on a grill rack in the oven for 5 minutes to get crispy garlic bulb.

Nutritional Value:

- Calories 8
- Total Fat 0 g
- Saturated Fat 0 g
- Cholesterol 0 mg
- Sodium 0 mg
- Total Carbs 1.5 g
- Fiber 0 g
- Sugar 0 g
- Protein 0 g
- Potassium 0 mg

ROASTED WHOLE GARLIC WITH HERBED BUTTER

Preparation Time: 5 minutes
Cooking Time: 20 minutes
Servings: 6

Ingredients:

- 3 large garlic bulbs
- 1 cup water
- 1 tablespoons herbed butter

Method:

1. Slice off ¼ of the garlic bulb from the top keeping the bulb intact.
2. Prepare the pressure cooker pot by adding water and place the rack on it.
3. Keep the garlic bulb on the rack and pressure cook for 5-6 minutes on high pressure.
4. Do a natural pressure release and remove the soft garlic very carefully. Apply the herbed butter on the garlic bulb.
5. Keep this in on a grill rack in the oven for 5 minutes to get crispy garlic bulb.

Nutritional Value:

- Calories 28
- Total Fat 1.5 g
- Saturated Fat 0.7 g
- Cholesterol 6 mg
- Sodium 18 mg
- Total Carbs 1.7 g
- Fiber 0 g
- Sugar 0.1 g
- Protein 1.4 g
- Potassium 0 mg

CARAMELIZED ONION

Preparation Time: 5 minutes
Cooking Time: 15 minutes
Servings: 4

Ingredients:

- 3 large onion bulbs
- 1 cup water

Method:

1. Slice off ¼ of the onion bulb from the top, keeping the bulb intact.
2. Prepare the pressure cooker pot by adding water and place the rack on it.
3. Keep the onion bulb on the rack and pressure cook for 5-6 minutes on high pressure.
4. Do a natural pressure release and remove the soft onion very carefully.
5. Keep this onion bulb on a grill rack in the oven for 5 minutes to get crispy browned onion bulb.

Nutritional Value:

- *Calories 6*
- *Total Fat 0 g*
- *Saturated Fat 0 g*
- *Cholesterol 0 mg*
- *Sodium 3 mg*
- *Total Carbs 1.4 g*
- *Fiber 0.5g*
- *Sugar 0.4 g*
- *Protein 0.2 g*
- *Potassium 26 mg*

PRESSURE COOKED ONION WITH HERBED BUTTER

Preparation Time: 5 minutes
Cooking Time: 15 minutes
Servings: 6

Ingredients:

- 3 large onion bulbs
- 1 cup water
- Herb butter, for rubbing onion

Method:

1. Slice off ¼ of the onion bulb from the top keeping the bulb intact.
2. Prepare the pressure cooker pot by adding water and place the rack on it.
3. Keep the onion bulb on the rack and pressure cook for 5-6 minutes on high pressure.
4. Do a natural pressure release and remove the soft onion very carefully.
5. Keep this onion bulb on a grill rack in the oven for 5 minutes to get crispy browned onion bulb.

Nutritional Value:

- Calories 14
- Total Fat 0.5 g
- Saturated Fat 0.2 g
- Cholesterol 2 mg
- Sodium 11 mg
- Total Carbs 1.9 g
- Fiber 0.7 g
- Sugar 0.6 g
- Protein 0.9g
- Potassium 70 mg

STEAMED SWEET POTATOES

Preparation Time: 10 minutes
Cooking Time: 10 minutes
Servings: 6
Ingredients:

- 10 baby sweet potatoes
- 1½ cup water

Method:

1. Place 1½ cups water in the cooker pot and place the rack or metal trivet.
2. Wash and keep the sweet baby potatoes on the steamer rack.
3. Lock the lid and cook this on high pressure for 8-10 minutes.
4. Do a pressure release and remove the baby potatoes carefully.
5. Season with salt and pepper. For crispier potatoes place them in the oven on grill rack for 5 minutes.

Nutritional Value:

- *Calories 83*
- *Total Fat 0 g*
- *Saturated Fat 0 g*
- *Cholesterol 0 mg*
- *Sodium 25 mg*
- *Total Carbs 18.3 g*
- *Fiber 1.7 g*
- *Sugar 10 g*
- *Protein 1.7 g*
- *Potassium 333 mg*

PRESSURE COOKER POLENTA

Preparation Time: 5 minutes
Cooking Time: 10 minutes
Servings: 6

Ingredients:

- 2 cups polenta, coarse
- 8 cups water
- 2 teaspoons salt

Method:

1. Fill the electric pressure cooker with the water and bring this water to a boil.
2. Add salt and polenta flour to the boiling water.
3. Keep stirring this continuously and close the lid of the cooker pot.
4. Cook this on high pressure for 8 minutes.
5. Do a natural pressure release and check for the doneness of polenta.

Nutritional Value:

- *Calories 185*
- *Total Fat 0.5 g*
- *Saturated Fat 0 g*
- *Cholesterol 0 mg*
- *Sodium 787 mg*
- *Total Carbs 40.6 g*
- *Fiber 1.3g*
- *Sugar 0.5 g*
- *Protein 3.8g*
- *Potassium 3 mg*

CHAPTER 6: SOUPS AND SALADS

MIXED VEGGIE SOUP

Preparation Time: 10 minutes
Cooking Time: 15 minutes
Servings: 10
Ingredients:

- 2 tablespoons olive oil
- 1 carrot, peeled and minced
- 1 celery stalk, minced
- 1 small onion, minced
- 2 garlic cloves, minced
- 1 teaspoon dried sage, crushed
- 1 teaspoon dried rosemary, crushed
- 8-ounce fresh Portabella mushrooms, sliced
- 8-ounce fresh white mushrooms, sliced
- ½ cup red wine
- 2 carrots, peeled and chopped
- 2 sweet potatoes, peeled and chopped
- 1½ cups fresh green beans, trimmed and chopped
- 1 tablespoon balsamic vinegar
- 3 cups water
- 2 tablespoons potato flour
- ¼ cup water
- ½ teaspoon salt
- ½ teaspoon black pepper
- ¾ cup pearl onion

Method:
1. Pour the oil in the Instant Pot and select "Sauté".
2. Then add in the carrots, celery and onion and cook for about 2-3 minutes. Add garlic and herbs and cook for about 1 minute.

3. Next, add mushrooms and cook for about 4-5 minutes. Add the wine and cook for about 2 minutes, scraping the brown bits from the bottom.
4. Select "Cancel" and stir in the carrots, potatoes, green beans, vinegar and water. Next, secure the lid and cook under "Manual" and "High Pressure" for about 15 minutes.
5. Select "Cancel" and carefully do a quick release.
6. Meanwhile in a bowl, dissolve potato flour into water.
7. Remove the lid of Instant Pot and immediately, stir in potato flour mixture, salt, black pepper and pearl onion. Select "Sauté" and cook for about 1 minute.
8. Serve hot.

Nutritional Value:
- *Calories 124*
- *Total Fat 3.4 g*
- *Saturated Fat 0.5 g*
- *Cholesterol 0 mg*
- *Sodium 139 mg*
- *Total Carbs 20.2 g*
- *Fiber 4.1 g*
- *Sugar 4 g*
- *Protein 4.2 g*
- *Potassium 534 mg*

SMOKED PAPRIKA LENTIL SOUP

Preparation Time: 10 minutes
Cooking Time: 25 minutes
Servings: 6
Ingredients:

- 1 cup red lentils, rinsed, skinless
- 1 cup green/brown lentils, skinless, rinsed
- 1 medium onion, chopped finely
- 3 cloves garlic, minced
- 2 teaspoons cumin
- 1½ teaspoon smoked paprika
- 2 carrots, sliced
- 2 celery stalks
- 1 bunch spinach
- 8 cups water
- 1 teaspoon salt
- 1 teaspoon pepper

Method:

1. Take an electric pressure cooker and select sauté and add oil, garlic, onion, spices, carrots, and celery for 5 minutes until onion soften.
2. Stir in the lentils and add water to cover.
3. Lock the lid into place and allow it to cook on high pressure for 10 minutes on soup mode and then on sauté mode for 5 minutes.
4. Use quick release method to release the pressure and unlock the lid safely.
5. Add in the smoked paprika, cumin, salt and pepper and serve hot on a serving dish.

Nutritional Value:

- *Calories 179*
- *Total Fat 1.2 g*
- *Saturated Fat 0.1 g*

- Cholesterol 0 mg
- Sodium 466 mg
- Total Carbs 31.8 g
- Fiber 14.1 g
- Sugar 3.2g
- Protein 12.5 g
- Potassium 863 mg

ORZO SOUP WITH BUTTERNUT SQUASH

Preparation Time: 10 minutes
Cooking Time: 25 minutes
Servings: 2 ½ quart
Ingredients:

- 3 tablespoons butter
- ½ cup green onions, diced
- ½ cup celery, diced
- ½ carrots, diced
- 1 garlic clove, minced
- 1 (4.5 oz.) can diced roma tomatoes with juice
- ½ teaspoon Italian seasoning
- 1/8 teaspoon red pepper flakes
- ¼ teaspoon pepper, freshly grounded
- 1/8 teaspoon nutmeg, freshly grated
- 1 cup orzo, cooked
- 1½ lb. butternut squash, diced
- 2 tablespoons scallion, thinly sliced for garnish
- 2 cups water
- 1 teaspoon half and half

Method:

1. Melt butter in the electric pressure cooker and select the sauté mode while adding in the onions, celery and carrots. Add garlic and stir briefly.
2. Add canned tomatoes and squash. Also add nutmeg, red pepper flakes and Italian seasoning.
3. Select high pressure and cook time of 10 minutes on soup mode.
4. When you hear the beep sound, turn the pressure cooker off. Wait for 10 minutes before opening the lid by doing a Quick pressure release.
5. Puree the mixture until smooth and creamy. Select simmer and add orzo and allow it to cook.
6. Serve with a swirl of half and half and some sprinkled green onion thins.

Nutritional Value:

- Calories 217
- Total Fat 4.2 g
- Saturated Fat 2.3 g
- Cholesterol 10mg
- Sodium 46mg
- Total Carbs 43.8 g
- Fiber 6.3 g
- Sugar 7.3 g
- Protein 4.9g
- Potassium 950 mg

CAULIFLOWER SOUP

Preparation Time: 5 minutes
Cooking Time: 25 minutes
Servings: 6
Ingredients:

- 2 tablespoons extra virgin olive oil
- 1 onion, chopped
- 2 teaspoons ginger, freshly chopped
- 2 garlic cloves, chopped
- 2 bunch cauliflower, florets only
- 2 teaspoons curry powder
- 1 teaspoon cumin
- ½ teaspoon salt
- 2 cups coconut milk
- 6 cups vegetable stock
- Few leaves coriander
- 4 almonds, blanched and sliced

Method:

1. Put olive oil in the pressure cooker and add in the onions while selecting the sauté mode in it, for 2-3 minutes.
2. Next add in the garlic cloves, ginger and cauliflower florets and allow it to sauté for 4 minutes.
3. Add in the spices such as cumin and salt.
4. Next, add in the almond milk along with vegetable stock and pressure cook it for 10 minutes by selecting the soup mode.
5. After the timer goes off, press cancel and quick release the pressure naturally and open the lid.
6. Puree the soup until it gets a smooth consistency.
7. Transfer the soup into the serving bowls topped up with coriander leaves and blanched almonds.
8. Enjoy eating.

Nutritional Value:

- Calories 260
- Total Fat 24.5 g
- Saturated Fat 17.6 g
- Cholesterol 0 mg
- Sodium 272 mg
- Total Carbs 10.1 g
- Fiber 3.7 g
- Sugar 4.8 g
- Protein 3.9 g
- Potassium 289mg

EASY NOODLE SOUP

Preparation Time: 10 minutes
Cooking Time: 30 minutes
Servings: 4
Ingredients:

- ¼ cup sesame oil
- 1 onion, julienned
- 2 teaspoons ginger, julienned
- 2 cans Portobello mushrooms, sliced
- 4 baby bok choy, thinly sliced
- 4 cups vegetable stock
- 12 oz raw shrimps
- 1 packet miracle noodles, boiled and rinsed
- 3 tablespoons coconut amino
- 5-6 lemon wedges

Method:

1. In an electric pressure cooker add in some oil and put in chopped onions; select the sauté mode and allow it to cook for 5 minutes.
2. Next put ginger, mushrooms and bok choy in it and give it a good mix for 2 minutes.
3. Now, add in the vegetable broth and shrimps in it, and cover the electric cooker with the lid; allow it to cook for 20 minutes on soup mode.
4. After the timer goes off, quick release the pressure naturally and pen the lid.
5. Now, add in the miracle noodles and let it cook for another 2 minutes.
6. Transfer the soup in the serving bowl and enjoy eating while serving it with lemon wedges.

Nutritional Value:

- *Calories 512*
- *Total Fat 30.6 g*
- *Saturated Fat 4.8 g*

- Cholesterol 358 mg
- Sodium 536 mg
- Total Carbs 16 g
- Fiber 4.2 g
- Sugar4.6 g
- Protein 43.9 g
- Potassium 787 mg

BROCCOLI CHEDDAR SOUP

Preparation Time: 5 minutes
Cooking Time: 20 minutes
Servings: 4
Ingredients:

- ¼ cup extra virgin olive oil
- 1 yellow onion, minced
- 2 celery, diced
- 3 cloves garlic, minced
- 1 teaspoon salt
- 1 teaspoon black pepper
- 2 cups broccoli, florets
- 1 cup coconut cream
- 2 cups vegetable broth
- 1 cup goat's milk cheddar cheese

Method:

1. In a pressure cooker put in some oil along with yellow onion and sauté it for 5 minutes.
2. Next, add in the celery ribs, garlic cloves, and salt, pepper and broccoli florets in it and give it a good mix.
3. Now, add in the coconut cream along with vegetable broth.
4. Close the lid of the cooker and pressure cook it for 15 minutes on soup mode.
5. After the timer goes off, quick release the pressure naturally.
6. Now add in the cheddar cheese and cook it for another 1 minute.
7. Transfer it in the serving bowl and enjoy eating.

Nutritional Value:

- *Calories 322*
- *Total Fat 29.6 g*
- *Saturated Fat 15.8 g*
- *Cholesterol 5 mg*

- *Sodium 1044 mg*
- *Total Carbs 11.1 g*
- *Fiber 3.3 g*
- *Sugar 4.4 g*
- *Protein 7.6 g*
- *Potassium 471 mg*

ASPARAGUS SALAD

Preparation Time: 10 minutes
Cooking Time: 20 minutes
Servings: 4

Ingredients:

- 1 lemon juice
- 2 salmon fillets
- 1 tablespoon champagne vinegar
- 1 tablespoons walnut oil
- 1 tablespoon Dijon mustard
- ¼ cup goat parmesan cheese, shredded
- ¼ cup fresh mint
- ¼ cup pine nuts, roasted
- ¼ teaspoon pepper
- 2 cups asparagus, shaved

Method:

1. Season the salmon with salt and set aside.
2. Next, take the electric pressure cooker and place a trivet inside it.
3. Place the salmon over the steamer rack and pressure cook it for 15 minutes.
4. After the timer goes off, quick release the pressure naturally and open the lid.
5. Transfer the salmon onto the plate and set aside.
6. In a serving plate put all the salmon and the asparagus and set aside.
7. In a small bowl put some lemon juice along with walnut oil, mustard, champagne vinegar, and give it a good whisk.
8. Drizzle the dressing over the raw asparagus and garnish it with pine nuts, pepper, mint and cheddar cheese.

Nutritional Value:

- *Calories 323*
- *Total Fat 21.7 g*
- *Saturated Fat 7.6 g*

- *Cholesterol 65 mg*
- *Sodium 176 mg*
- *Total Carbs 5.5 g*
- *Fiber 2.5 g*
- *Sugar 2.4 g*
- *Protein 28.5 g*
- *Potassium 601 mg*

FALL KALE SALAD

Preparation Time: 10 minutes
Cooking Time: 20 minutes
Servings: 6
Ingredients:

- 1 lemon juice
- 2 salmon fillets
- ¼ cup extra virgin oil
- 1 teaspoon Dijon mustard
- I tablespoon red wine vinegar
- 4 cups kale, thinly sliced, ribs removed
- 1 teaspoon salt
- 1 avocado, diced
- 1 cup pomegranate seeds
- 1 cup walnuts, toasted
- 1 cup goat parmesan cheese, shredded

Method:

1. Season the salmon with salt and set aside.
2. Next, take the electric pressure cooker and place a trivet inside it.
3. Place the salmon over the steamer rack and pressure cook it for 15 minutes.
4. After the timer goes off, quick release the pressure naturally and open the lid.
5. Transfer the salmon onto the plate and set aside.
6. In a bowl take some kale and season it with salt; set aside.
7. In another bowl make the dressing for the salad by combining lemon juice with olive oil, Dijon mustard and red wine vinegar.
8. Season kale with the dressing and add in the diced avocado, pomegranate seeds, walnuts and parmesan cheese.
9. Give it a good toss and serve it in a platter.

Nutritional Value:

- *Calories 234*

- Total Fat 14.3 g
- Saturated Fat 2.9 g
- Cholesterol 30 mg
- Sodium 490 mg
- Total Carbs 12.6 g
- Fiber 3.5 g
- Sugar 2.5 g
- Protein 16 g
- Potassium 654 mg

SEED-SAR SALAD

Preparation Time: 20 minutes
Cooking Time: 20 minutes
Servings: 4
Ingredients:

- 10 oz romaine leaves, washed thoroughly
- 2 salmon fillets
- 2 cups cocktail shrimps, cooked
- 12 oz crab meat
- 1 cup raw pumpkin seeds
- 2 garlic cloves, crushed
- ½ teaspoons sea salt
- ½ teaspoon black pepper, cracked
- 1 lemon juice
- 2 teaspoons Dijon mustard
- ½ cup goat parmesan cheese, shredded
- 8 tablespoons extra-virgin olive oil

Method:

1. Season the salmon with salt and set aside.
2. Next, take the electric pressure cooker and place a trivet inside it.
3. Place the salmon over the steamer rack and pressure cook it for 15 minutes.
4. After the timer goes off, quick release the pressure naturally and open the lid.
5. Transfer the salmon onto the plate and set aside.
6. In a food processor add in the raw pumpkin seeds, garlic cloves, sea salt, black pepper, and lemon juice, Dijon mustard plus olive oil and blend until a smooth puree is formed.
7. Next, place the romaine leaves on a serving platter and drizzle the dressing over it; mix until all the leaves are coated.
8. Serve it with shrimps and crab meat over the top along with cheese and freshly grounded pepper.

Nutritional Value:

- Calories 732
- Total Fat 34.3 g
- Saturated Fat 5.3 g
- Cholesterol 97 mg
- Sodium 693 mg
- Total Carbs 7.1 g
- Fiber 1.3 g
- Sugar 0.7 g
- Protein 27.3 g
- Potassium 490 mg

CHAPTER 7: SEAFOOD

SALMON CAKES

Preparation Time: 10 minutes
Cooking Time: 20 minutes
Servings: 8

Ingredients:

- 24 oz salmon, canned
- 4 teaspoons primal palate seafood seasoning
- ½ cup Vidalia onion, minced
- 6 pasture egg yolks
- 6 tablespoons organic palm oil, shortenings
- 2 teaspoons chives , garnish
- 4 teaspoons parsley, garnish
- 8 lemon wedges, for garnish

Method:

1. In a bowl take salmon along with egg yolks and seafood seasoning and combine them well.
2. Next, add in the minced onion and mix to combine all the ingredients.
3. Make small patties out of the mixture with 2-inch thickness each and set them on a baking tray or any heat proof tray.
4. Now, take an electric pressure cooker and place a trivet in it with almost 2 inch thickness.
5. Next, place the baking tray/ heat proof tray in the pressure cooker while closing the lid and setting the temperature on Manual high for almost 15 minutes.
6. After the time goes off, quick release the pressure naturally and open the lid.
7. Transfer the patties onto a tray.
8. Take a skillet and put some palm oil shortenings in it over a medium-high stove.
9. Next, place the patties over it, turning the sides until golden brown.
10. Transfer them on the plate and serve them with the garnish of lemon wedges, parsley and chives.

Nutritional Value:

- Calories 248
- Total Fat 18.8 g
- Saturated Fat 7 g
- Cholesterol 192 mg
- Sodium 44 mg
- Total Carbs 1.8 g
- Fiber 0.4 g
- Sugar 0.6 g
- Protein 18.7 g
- Potassium 365 mg

ADOBO SALMON SALAD WITH AVOCADO SALSA

Preparation Time: 20 minutes
Cooking Time: 10 minutes
Servings: 4
Ingredients:

- ¼ teaspoon sea salt
- 3 tablespoons green onion, sliced
- 1 ½ teaspoon jalapeno pepper, raw, seeded and minced
- 1 lb(4 filets) wild salmon filet
- 1 teaspoon extra virgin olive oil
- 1 teaspoon primal palate adobo seasoning
- 1 whole avocado, diced
- ¼ cup cilantro, minced
- ½ lime, juice
- 1/8 teaspoon black pepper, freshly grounded

Method:

1. Marinate the salmon with the olive oil and adobo seasoning and set aside.
2. Take a pressure cooker and place a steamer rack in it.
3. Next, place the salmon fillets over the rack and allow it to cook for 5 minutes under pressure by closing the lid of the electric pressure cooker.
4. After the time goes off, depressurize the cooker naturally and remove the lid from the top.
5. Now, take out the salmon fillets and place them on a cooling rack.
6. Take a bowl and combine together the avocado, lime juice, cilantro, sliced green onion, and jalapeno pepper, salt and freshly grounded pepper; set aside.
7. Place the salmon fillets on the serving plate and all the mixed greens over the top and enjoy eating.

Nutritional Value:

- *Calories 220*

- Total Fat 12.9 g
- Saturated Fat 1.8 g
- Cholesterol 55 mg
- Sodium 216 mg
- Total Carbs 3.3 g
- Fiber 1.9 g
- Sugar 0.3 g
- Protein 24.9 g
- Potassium 636 mg

PALEO SHRIMPS ON LETTUCE LEAVES

Preparation Time: 15 minutes
Cooking Time: 8 minutes
Servings: 4
Ingredients:

- 1 teaspoon primal palate taco seasoning
- 24 wholes raw shrimps, thawed, peeled and deveined
- 2 teaspoons extra virgin olive oil
- 2 cups romaine lettuce, shredded
- 1 whole radish, thinly sliced
- ½ avocado, diced
- ½ cup cilantro, chopped
- 1 whole roma tomato, diced, seedless
- 1 whole lime wedges, garnish
- 8 whole large lettuce leaves

Method:

1. Marinate the shrimps with the olive oil and the taco seasoning.
2. Place the steamer rack inside the electric pressure cooker and place the shrimps on it.
3. Cover it with the lid and pressure cook it for 3 minutes on high heat.
4. Next, when the timer goes off depressurize the cooker naturally and remove the lid.
5. Carefully transfer the shrimps onto a cooling rack.
6. Next, in a bowl take, cilantro, diced tomatoes, and romaine lettuce.
7. Now assemble everything on the lettuce leaves and enjoy eating.

Nutritional Value:

- *Calories 174*
- *Total Fat 8.5 g*
- *Saturated Fat 1.4 g*
- *Cholesterol 154 mg*

- Sodium 151 mg
- Total Carbs 5.4 g
- Fiber 2.6 g
- Sugar 1.4 g
- Protein 21 g
- Potassium 255 mg

SALMON BOWLS ASIAN STYLE

Preparation Time: 20 minutes
Cooking Time: 25 minutes
Servings: 4
Ingredients:

- 2 cups celery, chopped
- ¼ teaspoon garlic
- ¼ teaspoon ginger
- ¼ teaspoon red pepper flakes
- 4 cups white mushrooms, thinly sliced
- 1 tablespoon extra virgin olive oil
- 1 ½ lb wild caught salmon, fillet
- ¼ teaspoon Himalayan pink salt
- ½ teaspoon fish sauce
- 4 tablespoons coconut aminos
- 2 teaspoons sesame oil, toasted
- 4 tablespoons green onion, sliced
- 6 cups cauliflower, head only, grated
- ¼ teaspoon salt
- ¼ teaspoon pepper
- 2 tablespoons ghee

Method:

1. Marinate salmon with ginger, garlic, olive oil, and red pepper flakes; set aside.
2. Next, take a pressure cooker and place a steamer rack in it; place the salmon fillets on it.
3. Now, cover the pressure cooker with the lid to cook it on high pressure for about 25 minutes after selecting the manual button.
4. Meanwhile, place a wok on the stove over a medium high heat and put in the mushrooms along with celery and season them with salt and pepper; keep on frying.

5. Now add in the grated cauliflower head along with green onion, fish sauce, coconut amino, sesame oil, garlic powder and ginger.
6. When the timer goes off, depressurize the cooker naturally and take out the salmon from it and place it onto a cutting board.
7. Shred the salmon using two forks.
8. Transfer the salmon into the serving bowl along with the other ingredients and after tossing them all enjoy you eat!

Nutritional Value:
- Calories 351
- Total Fat 20.3 g
- Saturated Fat 5.9 g
- Cholesterol 72 mg
- Sodium 558 mg
- Total Carbs 15.5 g
- Fiber 5.5 g
- Sugar 5.7 g
- Protein 30 g
- Potassium 1314 mg

SHRIMP TACOS WITH POMEGRANATE SALSA

Preparation Time: 30 minutes
Cooking Time: 10 minutes
Servings: 4

- 1 lb raw shrimp, large, peeled and deveined
- 1 teaspoon primal palate jerk seasoning
- 1 tablespoon extra virgin olive oil
- 1 cup vine ripened tomato, seedless, diced
- 2/3 cup mango, peeled, and diced
- 2 tablespoons red onion, finely diced
- 1/3 cup pomegranate seeds
- 1 tablespoon lime juice
- ¼ teaspoon salt
- ¼ teaspoon cilantro
- 2 cups romaine lettuce, shredded
- 4 cassava flour tortillas

Method:
1. Season the shrimps with the jerk seasoning and set aside.
2. Place a steamer rack in the electric pressure cooker and pressure cook the shrimps in it for 3 minutes while covering it with lid.
3. Next, after the timer goes off, depressurize the cooker naturally and open the lid.
4. Transfer the shrimps onto a cooling rack.
5. Next, take a mixing bowl and place the pomegranate seeds, mango, tomato, and red onion in it along with drizzle of olive oil, lime juice, salt and chopped cilantro.
6. Warm the tortillas over the burner and assemble the tacos by placing the shrimps over the tortillas along with the pomegranate salsa.

Nutritional Value:
- *Calories 263*
- *Total Fat 6.4 g*
- *Saturated Fat 1.2 g*

- Cholesterol 239 mg
- Sodium 443 mg
- Total Carbs 23.5 g
- Fiber 2.9 g
- Sugar 6.9 g
- Protein 28.3 g
- Potassium 446 mg

STEAMED COD WITH HERBS AND LEMON

Preparation Time: 15 minutes
Cooking Time: 25 minutes
Servings: 4

Ingredients:

- 2 teaspoons primal palate amore seasoning
- ¼ teaspoon salt
- ¼ teaspoon pepper
- 2 tablespoons extra virgin olive oil
- 4 garlic cloves, minced
- 4 tablespoons clarified butter
- 16 oz cod, wild, two whole filets
- 2 lemon, juice only
- ½ cup parsley, chopped

Method:

1. Season the cod with salt and set aside.
2. Put some ghee in the electric pressure cooker and alongside with some olive oil and some onions and select the sauté mode for 4 minutes.
3. Add in the garlic and lemon juice and cook it further for 2 minutes.
4. Next, add in the amore seasoning to the sauce and cook it further for 2 minutes.
5. Place a steamer rack in the electric pressure cooker and place the fillets over it and cook it on high pressure for about 5 minutes.
6. After the timer goes off, quick release the pressure and open the lid.
7. Transfer the cooked cod along with the sauce in a serving platter topped up with chopped parsley and lemon wedges.

Nutritional Value:

- *Calories 297*
- *Total Fat 19.7 g*
- *Saturated Fat 8.5 g*
- *Cholesterol 93 mg*

- Sodium 243 mg
- Total Carbs 4.3 g
- Fiber 1.2 g
- Sugar 0.8 g
- Protein 26.8g
- Potassium 375 mg

COD WITH CITRUS AND FENNEL SALAD

Preparation Time: 10 minutes
Cooking Time: 10 minutes
Servings: 2
Ingredients:

- 2 cod fillets
- 1 lemon juice
- 1 tablespoon red wine vinegar
- 1 tablespoon extra-virgin olive oil
- 1 garlic clove, crushed
- 1 teaspoon Dijon mustard
- 1 red onion, julienned
- ½ bulb fennel, julienned
- 1 orange, small, fragments
- 2 cups baby spinach, rinsed thoroughly
- 1 cup pistachios, shelled
- 2 tablespoons orange zest

Method:

1. Season the cod with salt and set aside.
2. Next, take the electric pressure cooker and place a trivet inside it.
3. Place the cod over the steamer rack and pressure cook it for 15 minutes.
4. After the timer goes off, quick release the pressure naturally and open the lid.
5. Transfer the cod onto the plate and set aside.
6. In a bowl add in the lemon juice with red wine vinegar, extra virgin olive oil, garlic clove, and Dijon mustard; mix and set aside.
7. Next, in another bowl add in the red onion along with fennel, orange fragments, baby spinach, pistachios and orange zest.
8. Mix together the spinach with the dressing until the salad is evenly coated and serve onto the serving platter over the salmon fillets.

Nutritional Value:

- Calories 417
- Total Fat 22.7g
- Saturated Fat 2.7 g
- Cholesterol 50 mg
- Sodium 315 mg
- Total Carbs 32 g
- Fiber 9.7 g
- Sugar 13.6 g
- Protein 29.6 g
- Potassium 1023 mg

CHAPTER 8: POULTRY RECIPES
FETTUCCINE ALFREDO

Preparation Time: 30 minutes
Cooking Time: 30 minutes
Servings: 10
Ingredients:

- 1 teaspoon sea salt
- 1 teaspoon black pepper
- 5 packs shirataki fettuccine noodles
- 10 ounces shiitake mushrooms, sliced
- 2 bunches asparagus, trimmed and cut into 2-inch pieces
- 8 tablespoons Italian butter, salted
- 2 cans coconut cream, unsweetened
- 3 cups Parmigiano-Reggiano, grated
- 1 cup parsley, fresh, chopped
- 1 teaspoon Italian seasoning
- 1 lemon, zest only
- 2 cups water
- 1 lb pasteurized chicken, cut into small cubes

Method:

1. In an electric pressure cooker select the sauté mode and add in the butter and chicken and cook it for 2 minutes.
2. Now, add in the mushrooms and stir in for 2 minutes.
3. Next, put in the asparagus and stir for 2 minutes.
4. Now, add in the coconut cream and parmigiana into the sauce along with lemon zest, parsley, Italian seasoning and give it a good whisk.
5. Finally add in the fettuccine noodles along with 2 cups of water and close the lid of the pressure cooker.
6. Allow the noodles to get pressured cook for 14 minutes on manual.
7. After the timer goes off, quick release the pressure naturally and open the lid.

8. Finally select the "slow mode" till the alfredo is fully cooked and the sauce has thickened.

9. Serve the yummy pasta over a serving dish and enjoy while it's hot!

Nutritional Value:

- Calories 478
- Total Fat 15.6 g
- Saturated Fat 10.2 g
- Cholesterol 110 mg
- Sodium 473 mg
- Total Carbs 49.2 g
- Fiber 1.6 g
- Sugar 17 g
- Protein 37.2 g
- Potassium 382 mg

CHICKEN AND SPINACH QUICHE

Preparation Time: 10 minutes
Cooking Time: 20 minutes
Servings: 6
Ingredients:

- 12 large pasture eggs
- ½ cup coconut milk
- ½ teaspoon sea salt
- ¼ teaspoon ground pepper
- 3 cups fresh baby spinach, roughly chopped
- 1 cup pasteurize chicken pieces, chopped, diced
- 3 large green onions, sliced
- 4 green onion slices, topping the quiche
- ¼ cup goat cheese, shredded

Method:

1. In a large mixing bowl, whisk eggs, milk, salt, pepper.
2. Add onions, chicken pieces, chopped spinach leaves in a baking quiche mound. Pour the egg mixture from the top.
3. Garnish with green onion slices and grated goat cheese.
4. In an electric cooker pot, add 1½ cup water and put a steamer rack in it.
5. Next, place the quiche mound on the rack or the metal trivet.
6. Lock the cooker lid and cook on high pressure for 20 minutes. Leave it aside for 10 minutes.
7. Do a pressure release and remove the quiche and serve hot.

Nutritional Value:

- *Calories 249*
- *Total Fat 15.3 g*
- *Saturated Fat 7.8 g*
- *Cholesterol 457 mg*
- *Sodium 366 mg*

- Total Carbs 4.7 g
- Fiber 1.1 g
- Sugar 1.1 g
- Protein 23.2 g
- Potassium 235 mg

CHICKEN CEASE

Preparation Time: 10 minutes
Cooking Time: 30 minutes
Servings: 6
Ingredients:

- 2 tablespoons olive oil
- 2 kg pasteurize chicken breasts, boneless, skinless
- 1 cup chicken broth
- ½ cup Caesar salad dressing
- 4 cloves garlic, minced
- 1 tablespoon Italian seasoning, dried
- 1 cup broccoli florets, frozen, diced
- 1 cup cauliflower florets, diced
- 1 cup frozen carrots, peeled and diced
- ½ cup pimento stuffed olives, sliced
- ½ cup Parmigiano-Reggiano goat cheese

Method:

1. Heat olive oil in a pressure cooker pot and add chunk sized chicken pieces, cook water gets dried.
2. Stir broth, salad dressing, garlic and Italian seasoning mix.
3. Lock the lid and cook for 8 minutes.
4. Open the pressure cooker pot, add all the other remaining ingredients and cook on high pressure for 2 minutes.
5. Garnish with cheese before serving.

Nutritional Value:

- *Calories 337*
- *Total Fat 24.7 g*
- *Saturated Fat 10.2 g*
- *Cholesterol 74 mg*
- *Sodium 430mg*

- Total Carbs 10.2 g
- Fiber 1.3 g
- Sugar 3.9 g
- Protein 19.9 g
- Potassium 306 mg

CHICKEN TORTELLINI

Preparation Time: 10 minutes
Cooking Time: 25 minutes
Servings: 8
Ingredients:

- 3 slices bacon
- ¼ cup + 3 tablespoons grass fed butter
- 4 shallots, peeled and diced
- 1 tablespoon parsley, fresh
- 1 ½ kg pasteurized chicken breasts, boneless
- 1 small carrot, diced
- 1 (8 oz) package dried cheese tortellini
- 1 teaspoon tarragon leaves
- 2 cups rooster broth
- 1 lb asparagus
- 2 tablespoons all-purpose flour
- ¼ cup coconut milk
- ¼ cup heavy cream
- ½ cup hard goat cheese
- ½ teaspoon salt
- ½ teaspoon pepper, seasoning purpose

Method:

1. Fry the bacon till crisp and keep aside.
2. Stir in butter, shallots, parsley and sauté for 5 minutes.
3. Reduce the hen into bite sized chunk pieces; add carrot, tortellini, tarragon and broth. Stir well.
4. Cook this on high pressure for 6 minutes.
5. Do a quick pressure release and add 3 tablespoons butter mixed with flour to the cooker pot.
6. Whisk in milk and cream to the cooker pot, stir the cheese at the end, and cook this till the sauce is thickened.

7. Season with salt and pepper and serve hot.

Nutritional Value:

- Calories 468
- Total Fat 30.5g
- Saturated Fat 19.9 g
- Cholesterol 84 mg
- Sodium 989 mg
- Total Carbs 22.8 g
- Fiber 1.7 g
- Sugar 3 g
- Protein 26.9 g
- Potassium 216 mg

HERBED ROASTED WHOLE CHICKEN

Preparation Time: 10 minutes
Cooking Time: 25 minutes
Servings: 3
Ingredients:

- 8 lb pastured whole chicken
- ¼ teaspoon sea salt
- ¼ teaspoon black pepper
- ¼ teaspoon rosemary
- ¼ teaspoon thyme
- ¼ teaspoon oregano
- ½ cup pastured butter, diced
- 1 garlic bulb
- 1 orange, sliced
- ½ lemon, sliced

Method:

1. Take the whole chicken, season it with salt and fill in it with garlic bulb, orange slices and lemon slices; set aside.
2. Next, turn on the sauté mode of the electric pressure cooker and put in some butter; add in the chicken and keep on changing its side for 2 minutes.
3. Add in the spices along with some water and pressure cook it for 21 minutes.
4. Meanwhile preheat the oven at 370-degree Fahrenheit.
5. After the timer goes off, depressurize the electric cooker naturally and open the lid.
6. Put the chicken in the baking tray along with the left-over juices and place it in the oven for 15 minutes; just grill.
7. Serve the chicken in a serving platter along with baked sweet potatoes.

Nutritional Value:

- *Calories 463*
- *Total Fat 18.8 g*

- Saturated Fat 5.5 g
- Cholesterol 187 mg
- Sodium 1490 mg
- Total Carbs 27.9 g
- Fiber 4.8 g
- Sugar 6.1g
- Protein 43.4 g
- Potassium 136 mg

CHAPTER 9: BEEF, PORK, LAMB

BEEF INVENTORY

Preparation Time: 10 minutes
Cooking Time: 30 minutes
Servings: 6
Ingredients:

- 3 lb lean beef
- ½ lb carrots, chopped
- ½ lb onions, chopped
- ½ lb celery, chopped
- 1 tablespoon kosher salt
- ½ teaspoon black peppercorns
- Water

Method:

1. Mix all the ingredients in the pressure cooker pot along with water.
2. Add sufficient water to cowl all the ingredients.
3. Cook on high pressure for 20 minutes.
4. Do a natural pressure release and strain this inventory using cheesecloth.

Nutritional Value:

- *Calories 458*
- *Total Fat 14.2 g*
- *Saturated Fat 5.4 g*
- *Cholesterol 203 mg*
- *Sodium 1370 mg*
- *Total Carbs 8.5 g*
- *Fiber 2.4 g*
- *Sugar 4 g*
- *Protein 69.8 g*
- *Potassium 1190 mg*

FIERY BBQ MEAT BALLS

Preparation Time: 10 minutes
Cooking Time: 20 minutes
Servings: 8
Ingredients:

- 1 bag (48 oz.) beef meatballs, frozen fully cooked, grass fed beef
- 18 oz BBQ sauce
- 3-4 tablespoons Habanero Pepper Jelly
- 3 oz beef stock, grass fed beef

Method:

1. Add 1 cup water in pressure cooker
2. Add frozen meatballs to the steamer basket and pressure cook for 5 minutes on high.
3. When beeps, do a quick pressure release and remove the meatballs from electric cooker pot.
4. Discard cooking water and add BBQ sauce, beef broth and habanero pepper jelly to pressure cooker.
5. Select sauté; cook till the sauce is smooth.
6. Add heated meatballs and stir to combine.
7. Serve hot. Keep them warm until serving.

Nutritional Value:

- *Calories 146*
- *Total Fat 3 g*
- *Saturated Fat 1.1 g*
- *Cholesterol 19 mg*
- *Sodium 2642 mg*
- *Total Carbs 23.1 g*
- *Fiber 0.4 g*
- *Sugar 1.6g*
- *Protein 5.9 g*
- *Potassium 138 mg*

TACOS WITH BACON

Preparation Time: 10 minutes
Cooking Time: 20 minutes
Servings: 5
Ingredients:

- 2 tablespoons olive oil
- 1 lb cabbage, thinly shredded
- 8 oz bacon slices, browned and crispy, crumbled
- 4 green onions, chopped
- 2 tablespoons chili sauce
- 4 tablespoons sour cream
- ¼ cup onion
- ½ cup roma tomatoes, diced
- ¼ cup cilantro, chopped
- ¼ cup water
- 1 teaspoon salt
- 8 taco shells
- 1 avocado, peeled and sliced
- 1 cup goat cheddar cheese, shredded

Method:

1. Heat olive oil; add onions, tomatoes, cilantro, and salt.
2. Lock the lid and pressure cook this for 6 minutes on high pressure.
3. Unlock and remove the mixture in a bowl.
4. Take one taco shell, place spoonful of onion mixture cooked in pressure cooker, 2 tablespoons crumbled bacon, chili sauce, 2 teaspoons avocado slices, 2 teasp00ns sour cream, some shredded cabbage and chopped green onions and top them with shredded cheddar cheese and sour cream.

Nutritional Value:

- *Calories 394*
- *Total Fat 25.1 g*

- Saturated Fat 7.7 g
- Cholesterol 32 mg
- Sodium 1102 mg
- Total Carbs 29.3 g
- Fiber 4.5 g
- Sugar 4.5 g
- Protein 13.4g
- Potassium 447 mg

TACOS WITH HAM

Preparation Time: 10 minutes
Cooking Time: 20 minutes
Servings: 5
Ingredients:

- 2 tablespoons olive oil
- 1 lb cabbage, thinly shredded
- 8 oz Ham slices, browned and crispy, crumbled
- 4 green onions, chopped
- 2 tablespoons chili sauce
- 4 tablespoons sour cream
- ¼ cup onion
- ½ cup roma tomatoes, diced
- ¼ cup cilantro, chopped
- ¼ cup water
- 1 teaspoon salt
- 8 cassava flour taco shells
- 1 avocado, peeled and sliced
- 1 cup goat cheddar cheese, shredded

Method:
1. Heat olive oil; add onions, tomatoes, cilantro, and salt.
2. Lock the lid and pressure cook this for 6 minutes on high pressure.
3. Unlock and remove the mixture in a bowl.
4. Take one taco shell, place spoonful of onion mixture cooked in pressure cooker, 2 tablespoons crumbled Ham, chili sauce, 2 teaspoons avocado slices, 2 teasp00ns sour cream, some shredded cabbage and chopped green onions and top them with shredded cheddar cheese.

Nutritional Value:
- *Calories 586*
- *Total Fat 32 g*

- Saturated Fat 11.5 g
- Cholesterol 54 mg
- Sodium 2000 mg
- Total Carbs 54.7 g
- Fiber 8.5 g
- Sugar 7.4 g
- Protein 22.8 g
- Potassium 604 mg

BURRITO WITH PORK

Preparation Time: 10 minutes
Cooking Time: 20 minutes
Servings: 6
Ingredients:

- 2 tablespoons olive oil
- 8 oz pork pieces, browned and chopped
- 8 oz miracle rice, cooked
- ¼ cup onion
- ½ cup diced roma tomatoes,
- ¼ cup cilantro, chopped
- ¼ cup water
- 1 teaspoon salt
- 4 giant cassava flour tortillas
- 1 avocado, peeled and sliced
- Goat cheddar cheese, shredded

Method:

1. Heat olive oil; add pork pieces and stir fry till nicely browned. Add Miracle rice and mix together well. Remove and keep aside.
2. Add onions, tomatoes, cilantro and salt.
3. Lock the lid and pressure cook this for 6 minutes.
4. Unlock and remove the mixture in a bowl. Mix the rice and tofu mixture well.
5. Take one tortilla sheet, place spoonful of pork and rice mixture cooked in pressure cooker, 2 tablespoons of onion mixture, some avocado slices, shredded cheddar cheese and roll them tightly.
6. Cut them into small bites and serve with choice of sauce.

Nutritional Value:

- *Calories 114*
- *Total Fat 7.9 g*
- *Saturated Fat 2.4 g*

- Cholesterol 7 mg
- Sodium 77 mg
- Total Carbs 8.6 g
- Fiber 1.4 g
- Sugar 0.9 g
- Protein 3.2g
- Potassium 79 mg

STUFFED BACON IN ARTICHOKE

Preparation Time: 15 minutes
Cooking Time: 25 minutes
Servings: 4
Ingredients:

- 8 artichokes, medium sized
- 1 cup water
- 6 slices grass fed bacon, crumbled and cooked
- 1 cup goat cheese, crumbled
- 2 teaspoons salt
- 1 teaspoon pepper
- ½ teaspoon nutmeg powder
- 2 cups bread crumbs, lectin free
- 2 large pasture eggs
- 2 tablespoons olive oil

Method:

1. Clean and trim the artichokes well.
2. Place them upside down for opening and creating a hole or dent in the center.
3. In a mixing bowl, place all the above-mentioned ingredients and reserve half the cheese for using a topping. Lastly mix crumbled bacon to the mixture.
4. Take the artichokes and fill them well with this filling.
5. Garnish with the remaining half cheese.
6. Place the stuffed artichokes on the rack or the metal trivet. Cook this on high pressure for 5 to 7 minutes.
7. Do a quick pressure release and remove the stuffed artichokes on a serving platter.

Nutritional Value:

- *Calories 100*
- *Total Fat 2 g*
- *Saturated Fat 1 g*
- *Cholesterol 3 mg*

- Sodium 36 mg
- Total Carbs 18 g
- Fiber 2 g
- Sugar 11 g
- Protein 3 g
- Potassium 102 mg

MEAT LOVERS QUICHE

Preparation Time: 10 minutes
Cooking Time: 30 minutes
Servings: 6

Ingredients:

- 6 large pasture eggs
- ½ cup coconut milk
- ¼ teaspoon sea salt
- 1/8 teaspoon ground pepper
- 4 slices grass fed bacon, cooked and crumbles
- ½ cup grass fed ham, chopped
- ½ cup goat cheddar cheese, shredded

Method:

1. In a large mixing bowl, whisk eggs, milk, salt, pepper.
2. Add all the dry ingredients in a baking quiche mound. Pour the egg mixture from the top.
3. Garnish with crumbled bacon and grated cheddar cheese.
4. In a cooker pot, add 1 ½ cup water and place the rack. Place the quiche mound on the rack or the metal trivet.
5. Lock the cooker lid and cook on high pressure for 20 minutes. Leave it aside for 10 minutes.
6. Do a pressure release and remove the quiche and serve hot.

Nutritional Value:

- Calories 235
- Total Fat 18 g
- Saturated Fat 8.9 g
- Cholesterol 242 mg
- Sodium 686 mg
- Total Carbs 2.9 g
- Fiber 0.6 g

- Sugar 0.7 g
- Protein 15.2 g
- Potassium 181 mg

HAM FILLED EGG MUFFINS

Preparation Time: 10 minutes
Cooking Time: 2o minutes
Servings: 6

Ingredients:

- 4 pasture eggs
- ¼ teaspoon lemon pepper seasoning
- 4 tablespoons goat cheddar cheese, shredded
- 1 green onion, diced
- 4 slices grass-fed ham, precooked

Method:

1. Add 1½ cups water and place the rack in the cooker pot.
2. In a mixing bowl, break eggs and whisk well. Add all the other ingredients and divide the muffin batter equally in muffin mounds.
3. Place these muffins on the rack or metal trivet. Cook this on high pressure on 8 minutes.
4. Do a natural pressure release and remove the cooked muffins carefully.

Nutritional Value:

- *Calories 163*
- *Total Fat 11.3 g*
- *Saturated Fat 6.2 g*
- *Cholesterol 174 mg*
- *Sodium 353 mg*
- *Total Carbs 2.1 g*
- *Fiber 0.3 g*
- *Sugar 0.5 g*
- *Protein 12.9 g*
- *Potassium 71 mg*

BEEF STROGANOFF WITH MIRACLE NOODLES

Preparation Time: 10 minutes
Cooking Time: 30 minutes
Servings: 6

Ingredients:

- 2 lb grass fed pork sirloin tip roast
- ¼ teaspoon sea salt
- ¼ teaspoon pepper, freshly grounded
- 1 tablespoon olive oil
- 1 medium onion
- 1 cup dry white wine
- 1 tablespoon Dijon mustard
- 1 cup pasture chicken broth, low salt
- 1 tablespoon cassava flour
- 1 lb Portobello mushrooms
- 3 carrots
- 2 stalks celery
- ¼ cup goat cheddar cheese
- ¼ cup parsley, freshly chopped
- 12 oz miracle noodles

Method:

1. Toss the pork pieces with half teaspoon sea salt and pepper.
2. Heat oil in the pressure cooker, add the pork and cook stirring occasionally till sides are browned.
3. Add the onions, cook till soft, and now add dry white wine, mustard, flour. Bring this to simmer and cook till reduced half.
4. Add the chicken broth, celery, carrots and mushrooms.
5. Close the lid and bring to high pressure over medium heat and cook till 18 minutes.
6. Remove from heat using quick release method.
7. Stir in the cheese, parsley and remaining salt and pepper to taste.

8. Cook miracle noodles as per the instructions on the packet. Mix well in the pork stroganoff and serve.

Nutritional Value:
- Calories 376
- Total Fat 16.2 g
- Saturated Fat 9.3 g
- Cholesterol 82 mg
- Sodium 581 mg
- Total Carbs 22.1 g
- Fiber 3.7 g
- Sugar 4.2 g
- Protein 28.2g
- Potassium 341 mg

BRAISED PORK WITH ITALIAN SEASONING

Preparation Time: 15 minutes
Cooking Time: 35 minutes
Servings: 7

Ingredients:

- 3 lb grass fed pork loin, roasted
- 2 tablespoons olive oil
- 1 tablespoon Italian seasoning
- ¼ teaspoon salt
- ¼ teaspoon pepper

Method:

1. Rub the pork with salt, pepper and Italian seasoning.
2. Heat the olive oil and add the pork, cook till evenly browned.
3. Pour 1½ cups water and shut the lid. Cook for 25 minutes on high pressure.
4. Do a natural pressure release and then open the lid slowly.
5. Let the pork be relaxed for 5 minutes before slicing. Serve hot!

Nutritional Value:

- *Calories 511*
- *Total Fat 31.7 g*
- *Saturated Fat 10.8 g*
- *Cholesterol 157 mg*
- *Sodium 203 mg*
- *Total Carbs 0.3 g*
- *Fiber 0 g*
- *Sugar 0 g*
- *Protein 53.1 g*
- *Potassium 824 mg*

BRAISED PORK WITH MARINARA SAUCE

Preparation Time: 15 minutes
Cooking Time: 35 minutes
Servings: 7
Ingredients:

- 3 lb grass-fed pork loin roast
- 2 tablespoon olive oil
- 1 tablespoon Italian seasoning
- 1 cup marinara sauce
- ¼ teaspoon salt
- ¼ teaspoon pepper

Method:

1. Rub the pork with salt, pepper and Italian seasoning.
2. Heat the olive oil and add the pork, cook till evenly browned.
3. Pour 1½ cups water and shut the lid. Cook for 25 minutes on high pressure.
4. Do a natural pressure release and then open the lid slowly.
5. Add the marinara sauce and let the pork coat the sauce well.
6. Let the pork be relaxed for 5 minutes before slicing. Serve hot topped with marinara sauce from the cooker pot.

Nutritional Value:

- Calories 350
- Total Fat 12.4 g
- Saturated Fat 3.2 g
- Cholesterol 144 mg
- Sodium 339 mg
- Total Carbs 5.2 g
- Fiber 1 g
- Sugar 3.3 g
- Protein 51.5 g
- Potassium 933 mg

PORK WITH RISOTTO

Preparation Time: 15 minutes
Cooking Time: 30 minutes
Servings: 8
Ingredients:

- 6 bones in grass-fed pork chops
- 2 tablespoons grass-fed butter
- 1 cup miracle rice, dried
- 1 onion, chopped
- ½ cup red wine
- 1 tablespoon garlic, minced
- 1 lemon juice, zest
- 1½ cups grass-fed rooster broth
- 1/3 cup goat parmesan cheese

Method:

1. Warm the butter and add the pork chops and cook till nicely browned.
2. Stir within garlic and onion and cook dinner till softened, about 3 minutes.
3. Add the miracle rice and let it coat butter well.
4. Add red wine, lemon juice and zest to the miracle rice in the cooker pot.
5. Shut the cooker lid and cook on high pressure for 20 minutes.
6. Do a quick pressure release method.
7. Stir in goat parmesan cheese well and serve immediately.

Nutritional Value:

- *Calories 197*
- *Total Fat 8.5 g*
- *Saturated Fat 4 g*
- *Cholesterol 67 mg*
- *Sodium 440 mg*
- *Total Carbs 2.7 g*
- *Fiber 0.3 g*

- Sugar 1.2 g
- Protein 23 g
- Potassium 395 mg

CARNITAS

Preparation Time: 15 minutes
Cooking Time: 30 minutes
Servings: 8
Ingredients:

- 2½ grass-fed pork shoulders, chopped into ¾ inch pieces
- 1 teaspoon chipotle powder, dried
- ½ teaspoon cumin powder
- 1 big onion, chopped
- 2 cups low sodium pasture hen broth
- 10 cassava flour tortillas, toasted
- Guacamole
- Pico de Gallo
- ½ cup goat parmesan cheese, shredded

Method:

1. Combine all the ingredients in a pressure cooker pot and give it a stir so that ingredients get mixed well.
2. Next, pressure cook ingredients for half an hour and release the pressure naturally.
3. Shred the meat with two forks and mash onions with a masher.
4. Roast this shredded meat in the oven for about 10-12 minutes until the meat turns crispy.
5. Spoon this mixture of meat on roasted tortilla, along with Pico de Gallo, parmesan cheese and guacamole.
6. Serve these rolls immediately and enjoy eating!

Nutritional Value:

- *Calories 568*
- *Total Fat 38 g*
- *Saturated Fat 16.4 g*
- *Cholesterol 139 mg*

- Sodium 469 mg
- Total Carbs 14.9 g
- Fiber 2.2 g
- Sugar 1.3 g
- Protein 40.1 g
- Potassium 546 mg

LAMB WITH PORTOBELLO MUSHROOMS

Preparation Time: 10 minutes
Cooking Time: 30 minutes
Servings: 6
Ingredients:

- 2 lb grass-fed lamb chops
- 3 cans Portobello mushrooms
- 1 lb baby carrots
- 2 cups water
- 1 pack miracle noodles, cooked and buttered
- ¼ teaspoon salt
- ¼ teaspoon pepper

Method:

1. Empty the can of mushrooms in the pressure cooker pot.
2. Add water and stir well to combine.
3. Stir carrots and place the lamb chops in the pressure cooker.
4. Sprinkle with a touch of seasoning over it.
5. Lock the pressure cooker lid and cook this on high pressure for 20 minutes.
6. Release pressure and first serve the lamb chops, top them with carrots and the sauce from the cooker pot.

Nutritional Value:

- *Calories 287*
- *Total Fat 9.9 g*
- *Saturated Fat 3.5 g*
- *Cholesterol 120 mg*
- *Sodium 261 mg*
- *Total Carbs 8.1 g*
- *Fiber 2.7 g*
- *Sugar 3.6 g*
- *Protein 39.6 g*

- *Potassium 778 mg*

LAMB EMPANADAS

Preparation Time: 15 minutes
Cooking Time: 1 hour 20 minutes
Servings: 6
Ingredients:

- ½ cup red onion, diced
- 4 garlic cloves, chopped
- ½ poblano pepper, diced
- ½ cup fresh cilantro, chopped
- 3 lbs grass fed lamb meat, grounded
- 3 teaspoons Himalayan salt
- 4 teaspoons garlic powder
- 2 teaspoons black pepper, grounded
- 1 teaspoon oregano
- 2 teaspoons onion powder
- 14.5 oz roma tomatoes, blanched, peeled, deseeded and diced
- 10 Oz. goat cheddar cheese
- 6 almond flour empanadas
- 2 tablespoons grass-fed butter
- 1 large pasture egg, whisked for egg wash

Method:

1. Put some butter in the electric pressure cooker and add in the lamb beef, salt, garlic powder, black pepper, oregano, onion powder and mix; add in 2 cups of water and pressure cook lamb mince for 20 minutes.
2. After the timer goes off, depressurize the cooker naturally and open the lid carefully. Dry the water if any.
3. Preheat the oven at 400 degree Fahrenheit.
4. Next on the sauté mode and add in the onions and garlic cloves along with the lamb mince and give it a good mix for 10 minutes.
5. Now, add in the tomatoes and keep on mixing it for 10 minutes.
6. After that, add in the poblano pepper and keep on mixing it for 5 minutes.

7. Transfer the mixture onto a plate.
8. Fill each empanada with the mixture and fold it into semicircles and prick it from ends.
9. Coat each empanada with the egg wash and place them on a greased baking sheet.
10. Bake the empanadas for 10-15 minutes.
11. Take them out from the oven and serve it on a platter.
12. Enjoy eating!

Nutritional Value:
- *Calories 507*
- *Total Fat 4.1 g*
- *Saturated Fat 1.4 g*
- *Cholesterol 13 mg*
- *Sodium 61 mg*
- *Total Carbs 2.2 g*
- *Fiber 0.6 g*
- *Sugar 0.4 g*
- *Protein 3.7 g*
- *Potassium 40 mg*

CHAPTER 10: DESSERTS
FLOURLESS ALMOND CHOCOLATE CAKE

Preparation Time: 10 minutes
Cooking Time: 15 minutes
Servings: 1

Ingredients:

- 2 tablespoons swerve
- 2 tablespoons cocoa powder
- ¼ teaspoon baking powder
- 1 large pastured egg
- 1 teaspoon coconut cream
- ½ teaspoon vanilla extract
- ½ cup water
- 2 tablespoons almond butter

Method:

1. In a bowl mix all the dry ingredients sift and set aside.
2. In another bowl, mix all the wet ingredients and set aside.
3. Mix ingredients of both bowls and keep aside.
4. Grease a ramekin and pour the batter in it.
5. In an electric cooker place 1 cup of water and a trivet.
6. Place the ramekin over the trivet and close the lid to cook the cake on pressure for 15 minutes.
7. After the timer goes off, depressurize the cooker naturally and open the lid carefully.
8. Take out the ramekin from the pot and release the cake from the pot and place it on the platter.
9. Drizzle almond butter over it and serve hot or cold as desired.

Nutritional Value:

- *Calories 319*
- *Total Fat 25.1 g*

- Saturated Fat 4.8 g
- Cholesterol 215 mg
- Sodium 75 mg
- Total Carbs 18.1 g
- Fiber 6.6 g
- Sugar 2 g
- Protein 14.9 g
- Potassium 655 mg

CRANBERRY ORANGE MUFFINS

Preparation Time: 10 minutes
Cooking Time: 25 minutes
Servings: 2
Ingredients:

- ¼ teaspoon iodized sea salt, sifted
- ¼ tablespoon baking soda, sifted
- ¼ cup melted butter
- ¼ cup xylitol, sifted
- 3 large pastured eggs
- 2 tablespoons orange zest
- ½ cup cranberries, dried
- ¼ cup coconut flour, sifted

Method:

1. In a bowl put in the salt, along with coconut flour, xylitol and baking soda.
2. Next, add in the melted butter, eggs, orange zest and give it a good whisk.
3. Now, put in the fresh cranberries and fold them with a light hand.
4. Take a pressure cooker and put a trivet inside it along with 1 cup of water.
5. Grease the muffin tray and divide the batter among 4 mounds.
6. Place the muffin tray over the trivet and pressure cook it for 20 minutes after closing its lid.
7. After the timer goes off, quick release the pressure and open up the lid.
8. Finally release the muffins from the tray and serve.

Nutritional Value:

- *Calories 409*
- *Total Fat 31.3 g*
- *Saturated Fat 17.8 g*
- *Cholesterol 384 mg*
- *Sodium 1124 mg*
- *Total Carbs 20.6 g*

- Fiber 7.6 g
- Sugar 1 g
- Protein 11.4 g
- Potassium 66 mg

CHOCOLATE MINT BROWNIES

Preparation Time: 10 minutes
Cooking Time: 25 minutes
Servings: 4
Ingredients:

- ¼ cup macadamia nuts
- ¼ cup fresh mint
- ¼ teaspoon baking soda
- ½ cup coconut oil
- 3 ounces bittersweet chocolate, chunks
- 2 tablespoons erythritol
- 1 ½ tablespoon coconut flour
- 1 tablespoon peppermint extract
- 3 large pasture eggs

Method:

1. Take a food processor and add in the macadamia nuts, mint and baking soda in it; process.
2. Next, add in the coconut oil along with bittersweet chocolate, erythritol, coconut flour, omega eggs and peppermint extract; process again.
3. Grease a heat proof flat dish and pour the batter in it.
4. Take an electric pressure cooker and place a trivet in it; place the heat proof dish on the trivet and pressure cook the brownie bar after closing the lid of the cooker for 30 minutes almost.
5. After the timer goes off, quick release the pressure naturally and open the lid.
6. Next, release the bar from the mound and cut it into smaller chunks.
7. Serve it on the plate and enjoy eating.

Nutritional Value:

- *Calories 473*
- *Total Fat 43.3 g*
- *Saturated Fat 30.1 g*

- Cholesterol 166 mg
- Sodium 147 mg
- Total Carbs 23 g
- Fiber 1.8 g
- Sugar 19.2 g
- Protein 7 g
- Potassium 141 mg

MIRACLE RICE PUDDING

Preparation Time: 10 minutes
Cooking Time: 30 minutes
Servings: 5
Ingredients:

- ½ cup coconut oil, unsweetened
- 5 tablespoons arrowroot powder
- 3 cups coconut milk, unsweetened
- ¼ cup cocoa powder, non-alkalized
- 1 cup swerve
- 1 teaspoon ghee
- 1 teaspoon vanilla extract
- 1 pasteurized egg, whisked
- 2 bags miracle rice
- 1 cup water

Method:

1. Take an electric pressure cooker and put coconut milk in it along with, cocoa powder, swerve, ghee, vanilla extract, egg and 2 bags miracle rice; keep on stirring it for 10 minutes on the sauté mode.
2. Next, add in the coconut oil, arrowroot powder in it and further cook it until it gets a thick consistency.
3. Pour the batter onto a greased heat proof bowl and clean up the pressure cooker.
4. Place a trivet inside the clean cooker along with 1 cup water and the baking bowl on the trivet.
5. Close the lid and pressure cook the pudding for 20 minutes.
6. After the timer goes off, open the lid and take out the bowl carefully.
7. Serve hot.

Nutritional Value:

- *Calories 589*
- *Total Fat 58.4 g*

- *Saturated Fat 50.5 g*
- *Cholesterol 45 mg*
- *Sodium 37 mg*
- *Total Carbs 19.1 g*
- *Fiber 4.5 g*
- *Sugar 5 g*
- *Protein 5.3 g*
- *Potassium 488 mg*

CAULIFLOWER RICE PUDDING

Preparation Time: 10 minutes
Cooking Time: 30 minutes
Servings: 4
Ingredients:

- 1 lb cauliflower head, small, processed in food processor
- 3 cups coconut milk
- 1 cup coconut flakes, unsweetened, powdered
- 1 tablespoon vanilla extract, pure
- ½ teaspoon sea salt
- 1 teaspoon raw honey
- Pinch nutmeg

Method:

1. In an electric pressure cooker put some coconut oil and turn on the sauté mode.
2. Add in the cauliflower rice and give it a mix for 15 minutes.
3. Transfer it to a plate for further use.
4. Now in the same cooker pot add in some coconut milk along with vanilla, powdered coconut flakes, honey, salt and nutmeg; give it a good mix and allow it to cook for 15 minutes.
5. Finally add in the fried cauliflower rice into the coconut milk mixture and allow it to cook for 5 minutes, until thickened.
6. Serve it in a bowl and enjoy eating!

Nutritional Value:

- *Calories 528*
- *Total Fat 49.7 g*
- *Saturated Fat 44 g*
- *Cholesterol 0 mg*
- *Sodium 299 mg*
- *Total Carbs 20.9 g*
- *Fiber 8.6 g*

- *Sugar* 11.1 g
- *Protein* 7.1 g
- *Potassium* 894 mg

CONCLUSION

Lectins are considered to be harmful and are present mostly in the seeds of the plants. Apart from their harm, there is a considerable amount of research to support the consumption of plant related foods. The lectin levels in plants may vary from one to another according to the plant types. Most of the research done on lentils is mostly performed on animals and other test tube studies. Despite the fact that the majority of the researches have focused a specific lectin instead of the plant carrying it, it has yet been credited with the reason of many diseases and medical complications like inflammation and digestion issues.

92555706R00064

Made in the USA
Middletown, DE
09 October 2018